Pray W9-DFD-817

The White Paradise

by Peter van der Meer de Walcheren

with a preface by
Jacques Maritain

NEW YORK
DAVID McKAY COMPANY, INC.

This authorized translation is made from the original Dutch, *Het Witte Paradijs* (Utrecht: Uitgeverij Het Spectrum, 1948) by F. E. Holden.

MANUFACTURED IN THE UNITED STATES OF AMERICA BY THE
VAIL-BALLOU PRESS, INC., BINGHAMTON, N. Y.

CONTENTS

INTRODUCTION 11

1. THE MONASTERY IN THE MOUNTAINS . . 23

2. THE DESERT FATHERS 30

3. SAINT BRUNO 40

4. DAYS AND NIGHTS IN THE CHARTERHOUSE OF
   LA VALSAINTE 52

5. THE CARTHUSIANS AND OURSELVES . . . 66

6. A CARTHUSIAN SPEAKS 74

7. BACK IN THE WORLD 90

LIST OF ILLUSTRATIONS

	FACING PAGE
Saint Bruno	32
The Cloister	33
The Charterhouse of La Valsainte	48
Entrance to the Chapel	49
A Monk's Workshop	64
A Monk's Cell	65
A Cell Garden	80
The Cemetery	81

THE
WHITE PARADISE

INTRODUCTION

THE place was the Church of St. Medard, the date February 11, 1911. Few Parisians do not know the old St. Medard Quarter, that endearing short stretch of the Rue Mouffetard where, amid the smell of fish and the noise of the street vendors, one finds a terrible poverty, impressive as a relic, almost as ancient as old Paris itself, and weary poetic dreams which feed on revolution and mathematical vapors. . . . At the back of the dark church, before the baptismal font, a man and a small boy stood side by side, holding the same candle and beaming with joy: it was Pieter Matthias van der Meer de Walcheren and his son Pieter Leo who had just been born again of water and the Holy Spirit. The old godfather Léon Bloy was praying for them in the shadows, with the calm of a lion devouring his prey.

I had met Pieter and Christine van der Meer only a few weeks earlier at Léon Bloy's. Like ourselves six years before, they had come to ask the "Ungrateful Beggar" the way to Heaven. Since then a great many years have passed. How can I write of this great pure-hearted Hollander, how indeed am I to speak of a man

so simple, so straightforward—and so powerful a
writer, so profoundly poetic, so great a connoisseur of
the art and culture of Europe—if not as a matchless
friend and brother given me by the Lord? We have
lived through too many joys and sorrows together;
more sorrows than joys, in fact. "Yes, Pieter, we shall
have a few things to remember about this planet!"

It is not my purpose here to tell the story of Pieter
van der Meer's conversion. He has told it himself in
his admirable *Diary of a Convert*, which he wrote
in Dutch and later translated into French, with a preface by Léon Bloy. I wish only to put down a few of
the dates and facts of his life up to the present.

Born in Utrecht in 1880 and reared in an environ-
ment of refinement and culture much influenced by
Goethe, his was, to start out with, a heart and mind
torn with anxiety and impatience, and the desire for
that Beauty which he has called "the song of priva-
tion." Become a follower of Nietzsche and—naturally
—a revolutionary, it was at the "Maison du Peuple"
in Brussels that he was to meet his wife, at the time a
militant Socialist and utterly unaware, of course, that
she should one day be her husband's best helper in the
quest for things divine. He had already read a few of
Bloy's works, which his friend Alphonse Diepenbrock,
the composer, had given him, but his admiration for
Bloy was still merely literary.

At the age of twenty he had finished his studies at
the University of Amsterdam and received a degree in

classical philology. He left Holland, the prey of a restlessness whose cause he did not understand. He traveled in Germany, visiting Munich and Bayreuth, and went on to Vienna. In 1901, he made a first stay in Paris and wrote his first novel, *Jong Leven* (Young Lives). Then he married, in June, 1902, and settled at Uccle in Belgium, where he undertook the hazardous business of living by his pen, started several reviews and wrote short stories and novels—sad, tragic, spiritually barren works.[1] But no matter. One of his novels, *De Jacht naar Geluk*, ended with the Lord's Prayer.

Van der Meer had at last perceived the fact of Catholicism. First in Belgium, during a visit to the Trappist Monastery at Westmalle, then in Italy, he had encountered the Faith. Henceforth, his spiritual disquietude merely increased. Then came the years recounted in his *Diary*, ending with his baptism. On receiving his true name, he had found his place and his mission.

What had happened was something quite simple: he had taken his baptism seriously; he knew that the water through which God passes does not touch the forehead alone but the whole of a man's being, down to that last recess in the heart of man where art and poetry take hiding. He had given all—and that is what is pleasing to God. Something quite simple, indeed; but every-

[1] *Levens van Leed* (Lives of Sorrow), *Vreemde Verhalen* (Strange Tales) and *De Jacht naar Geluk* (The Search for Happiness).

thing was different now. Art and literature had also
to be buried with Christ in order to live again with
Him; had to consent to the death demanded by the
Gospel; had to agree to the loss of self. Farewell to
bluff and bravado! Farewell to the air of "knowing
all the answers," to the forces of pride, to popularity
with the "advance guard" and the "rear guard" as well,
to sensational entries into the beauty and wisdom of the
world! You now take the servants' entrance—the
entrance of the servants of God. Let God, if He will,
break open the doors and provide the strength. It was
from this primary consent, and this rebirth in God, that
came Van der Meer's quiet, radiating power; nor was
it long before he began exercising an influence upon
the youth of Holland.

Before this latter had occurred, however, there were
the four years of the Great War, during which he acted
as Paris war correspondent for the *Maasbode;* there
was the death of Léon Bloy, and there was the death of
a small child, opening up at once the sources of the
greatest suffering and the sources of the unseen paradise.

At the end of the war, Van der Meer took his family
to live in the small town of Oosterhout in Dutch Bra-
bant, so as to be near the Benedictine Abbey of which
his wife and he had become oblates—Saint Paul's of
Oosterhout, a foundation of Solesmes, a monastery
where, almost every Saturday in Holy Week, God

sends an adult to be baptized; and where young Pieter Leo already knew he would be a monk.

Then followed three years of work and prayer away from the eyes of the public; and Van der Meer produced, one after the other, a book of travel memories (*Italy*, treating of Pisa, Florence, Siena, Assisi, and Rome), the story of his conversion (*Mijn Dagboek*), a novel (*Van het verborgen Leven*—Within the Hidden Life), and a life of Saint Benedict. Toward the beginning of 1921, he was appointed literary and art editor of a weekly called *Nieuwe Eeuw*, and lived first in Helmond and then in Amsterdam, where he later directed the *Opgang* review.

With no intention on his part (that, one may be sure of!), his appearance amid the quiet life led by his Catholic fellow countrymen had the effect of a bolt from the blue. His task was first and foremost to assert the cultural power of Catholicism as something as alive and as valid as ever in the past. This sort of task involves going out and attacking the Devil where he is so much at home—I mean, in that place called Literature on the world's maps, where the Prince of this world holds garrison. Van der Meer's position here is the correct one. He does not make of art and literature an end in themselves; he loves them—with what intensity! But he loves them, before all else, for the sake of God.

To love painting, music, the novel, the films for God, that's paradoxical enough; but where does beauty, all beauty, come from, if not from God? And is not art here below an essential part, and, as it were, the worldly angel—that we utilize for both good and evil (the more often for evil, but this is not art's fault, it is the fault of the artist)—of this life of ours which is called by God to partake in His own life? To those who share Van der Meer's views, what is perhaps more interesting in the art of any period than the results actually achieved is the current of invention and creation which passes through time. This is why they are so readily sympathetic to all new artistic efforts. At the same time they remain all the more free with respect to these efforts, as in truth one thing only is of absolute importance for them—that God shall be loved and that souls shall be touched by the Blood of Christ.

It is not therefore difficult to understand that the young Catholic intellectuals of Holland, with the instinctive and inexorable movement of life in search of itself, should have grouped themselves in very little time around Pieter van der Meer. How many, indeed, are the souls that have been retempered by his peaceful and ardent faith! One particular thing he did was to turn his friends' attention in the direction of the great Catholic tradition of France, at the same time showing them how to distinguish the good from the bad in the incredible mass and mixture of the contemporary literary movement. Through his personal influence, as well as his writings—essays, articles, books—he succeeded in stirring up a whole generation and putting it to work.

As the Dutch writer, Jan Engleman, expressed it several years ago, "At the moment when life in Europe was entering into a sort of apocalyptic phase, Pieter van der Meer told the Dutch, and specially the Catholic Dutch, that it was no longer possible, no longer permissible to go on living as if nothing were happening in the world. This he did with his great passion for truth, in terms which, though laden with kindness and purity of intention, spared neither persons nor things. He was no doubt not entirely understood. Truths like those he uttered always take time to sink in, and are not always welcome, besides. People often fight against such a message, scoffing at the weak points which occur in the reaction it provokes and which they take as an excuse for a lordly disregard of its value. Considerable work had been done before him—as it has since—with a great deal of merit, in behalf of Christian-minded cultural tradition, which moreover is no longer denied. But he came at a time of uncertainty when, owing to events which could no longer be controlled, a link was missing in the chain of the tradition. We know of no one who has worked in this field with nobler intentions or a stronger desire for the victory of the supreme good. He exploded completely the false values upon which people were blindly resting. He showed that Catholic Holland had grown cold from the chill winds of a Calvinism destructive of all new cultural growth. He was thus responsible for more than one shock that upset habits of mind and judgment and, in all this, he

acted with a generosity so complete, and a powerful-
ness so winning, that there would be many a wonderful
story to tell of him were it not for the discretion one
owes him. . . ."

Well, after this period of deep and spreading activity,
the moment had necessarily to come when "another
shall gird thee, Peter, and carry thee where thou doest
not wish to go." Those who know Pieter and Christine
van der Meer know that if ever the natural and super-
natural fullness, the peaceful and fruitful exaltation and
the sanctifying power of human love and the sacrament
of marriage has been lived by two beings, it has been
lived by them. Nor is there anything surprising to their
friends in the fact that it was just here, here at the deep
source of life and experience, and in that splendor
which the children of benediction crowning their love
bring to such a father and such a mother, that the great
night of sacrifice should have made its regal entry.
They had given little Jean-François to Heaven. They
had given Pieter Leo to Saint Benedict. They now had
to give Anne-Marie likewise to Saint Benedict—Anne-
Marie, frail and fearless, full of promise in art and
literature; and she entered the Abbey of Our Lady of
Oosterhout on October 12, 1931. And then—

Pieter Leo had taken his vows in 1923, and been
ordained in 1929. Suddenly, less than four years later
—on February 2, 1933—death fell upon him as on a
gentle prey. Within the space of a few hours, one after

another, three telegrams, like three strokes of a sword, each more terrible, each cutting deeper, came and pierced Pieter and Christine's hearts: Pieter Leo was seriously ill; Pieter Leo had received extreme unction; Pieter Leo was dead.

They were soon to know something of the invisible marvels with which their son's grace of prayer, his complete abandonment to God, his monastic life, all-hidden, pure, generous and loving, with its extraordinary radiance—a radiation, moreover, which still continues to be active—had prepared him for the death of a chosen soul. But, for them, everything the world could bring, all experience, was finished and over; and here they were, thrust into that terrible solitude where the God who demands *all* seems to say: "It is not enough," and asks still more. This something more Pieter and Christine van der Meer did not refuse to give; they made the offering, the holocaust, of their own hearts by sacrificing the sacred bond between them which God had made identical with their lives themselves. And then, having seen their gift and its heroism, God, that same God who had at the end spared Abraham, gave them back to each other and sent them among us again.

Pieter returned to work, both as a writer and as a publisher. It was due to him, in this latter capacity, that Desclée de Brouwer in Paris underwent the remarkable development it did during the last several years before the Second World War. If he bears on his fore-head the luminous shadow of those whom the divine hand has marked with the sign of sorrow, his activity is but the more energetic and fruitful for it.

The White Paradise (*Het Witte Paradijs*) was first published in 1930, shortly before Van der Meer left Holland to settle in France. Because of the love and reverence I have, as he has, for the Carthusian life, because of the nostalgic memory I keep, as he keeps, of La Valsainte, it has been a particular joy for me to have been asked to write the preface for the translation of this book in which my friend has not only expressed so extraordinarily well the impressions felt by the passing pilgrim, but has also drawn, in some of its deepest features, the spiritual portrait of those men of solitude who remain all their lives in those heights, praying for us recalcitrant ingrates.

Postscriptum. I have held the conviction for a long time that beneath the fever of activity imposed by modern civilization there is in the American soul a profound need and a genuine capacity for contemplation and contemplative life. I have often expressed this conviction. I remember that many years ago I urged my Carthusian friends in France or in Italy to found a Charterhouse in this country. Now a number of signs are witnessing to this thirst for spiritual life which exists and develops in significant sections of American youth. It is not without special emotion that I see the

English edition of Pieter van der Meer's book appear at a moment when Carthusians have come to America.

On April 16, 1951, at a general chapter held at the Grande Chartreuse, the first American foundation was approved. A Spanish Carthusian prior and a professed monk had been sent from Spain to investigate offers of property here. They had chosen a spot in the mountains of Vermont where a recent convert to Catholicism had presented them with a farm of five hundred acres, a spot reminiscent in its mountain scenery of the site of the Grande Chartreuse, the motherhouse of the Order. After approval of the foundation the prior returned to Spain and an English monk was sent from England as superior of the new American foundation. Here in Vermont the monks have built small wooden houses in which the Carthusian life can be lived as in the days of Saint Bruno.

These newcomers have met the most generous response in this country from many who are opening their hearts more every day to the contemplative ideal. Many offers of aid have come to them from the most unexpected quarters and the number of applicants for admission to the Order has surpassed their more sanguine hopes, although the difficulties of the life may well limit the number who will actually be professed. These applicants are being sent abroad for training in the Carthusian life, and La Valsainte, the monastery described in Pieter van der Meer's pages, was among the first to receive them. It is then fitting that this book should now appear in English to give to others a glimpse of those high places where burns an invisible fire and where man and God meet and join in love and contemplation.

June, 1952   Jacques Maritain

I

THE MONASTERY
IN THE MOUNTAINS

THE second section of the Paris-Lausanne night-express in which we were traveling was delayed to the improbable extent of four and a half hours—"What have you done with your train, gentlemen?" was the Swiss conductor's joke. And so we missed all the connections we had so carefully worked out beforehand. But this turned out to be a good thing, for that was how we came to run through the Jura into Switzerland just as the sun, as pure and young as in the hour of creation, rose in a dawn that unfolded its light above the snow-clad mountains. From our warm little corner in the railway carriage we saw the world lying still and white and shining all round us.

And that, too, was how it came to be midday, a blue, sunny midday, when we ran for a while alongside the Lake of Geneva between sparse vineyards lightly powdered with snow which looked naked and barren, and gleamed against the hillsides like mysterious churchyards full of tombstones. Far behind the hills the great mountains heaved their stark, white flanks on high, mighty and lonely against the heaven of light.

After that the stuffy little electric train took us from Palézieux round fantastic curves deeper into the white mountains, sometimes stopping incredibly long at a little station behind which, presumably, there lay an invisible hamlet. Ever higher became the mountains, ever lonelier the valleys, ever deeper and more solid the snow.

We alighted at Bulle, a quiet, neat little town, almost terrifying in the busy narrowness of its life, like every other small provincial town the world over. By now it was late in the afternoon; the light was growing softer, and declining to evening. We wanted to be far away in the monastery before dark and before it was too late.

A motorcar. A ten-mile race with the twilight. At a dangerous speed the little car rushed over the road. In the distance, silhouetted against the evening sky, lay Gruyère, the mountain home of cheese. Then we came to the little town of Broc, where a sweet-smelling, chocolaty atmosphere assailed us.

The motor, with chains on the back wheels, sped in safety but with undiminished speed over the frozen, slippery snow. Night was falling. Who would win the race—we or the darkness?

Slipping at a giddy speed past deep abysses, past steep, sheer walls of rock, round abrupt bends in the road, we climbed to meet the solitude, rushed with noisy haste into the silence. The mountains looked like gigantic, rough crystals, and where the shadows fell across them—shadows vast enough to have been cast by another planet—they were of a steely blue color. One peak was glowing, and went on glowing marvelously in the light from the invisible sun, like a soul made bright with the grace of God.

Suddenly the chauffeur switched his lights on. The road grew narrower, with fir trees as high as houses on one side, and on the other a sullen-looking wall of rock. And round a bend the world burst upon us again in a magnificent glimpse of endless white valleys and endless white mountains. On, on sped the little growling car, searching out with the rays from its headlights the dangerous, ever mounting road, like a frenzied insect finding its way with its feelers.

It grew frightfully cold; the temperature was near zero. In the awful silence our car made the only sound there was—like a child, noisily afraid.

Suddenly a wall appeared as the two beams from our headlights were upon it. We swung past it in low gear, then stopped, and the chauffeur switched off the motor. We and the white night had arrived together.

The Carthusian Monastery of La Valsainte.

Only a short time ago, I had been standing amid the confusion and smells of Paris. Now I had suddenly been hurled, without transition, into the deepest, purest silence.

And there inside, behind that great door and the

enclosing walls, lived the monks in this silence. They
had not withdrawn into solitude for a few days, to find
themselves and to seek after God, but, weaned from
the world, they stood motionless all their life long, all
the days and all the nights, in the presence of a silence
that terrified me, the silence of the world of the spirit.

My companion rang the doorbell. A white monk
with a lantern in his hand opened the door. They were
expecting us. It was December 23rd.

Round the inner courtyard there were dark build-
ings, staring and expressionless like objects in a frozen
world. We crossed the courtyard with the snow
crunching under our feet and came to a cold, dark
house, the guest quarters. All the windowpanes were
opaque with frost. The cold lay its icy grip upon my
face, and I shuddered, like the child in the ice palace
of the Snow Queen. But here the heart did not freeze;
here there was no one seeking to spell out the word
ETERNITY in fragments of ice. They had found it here,
and God had burned up their hearts in His white-hot
fire.

Now, by the meager glimmer of an oil lamp, I could
see the Brother Porter's face—a tranquil, bearded face,
with the eyes of a child, as clear as the sky. He handed
us over to another monk, the Brother in charge of
guests, who welcomed us in a low voice and with a
trusting smile.

He led us up a wide, dark stairway through the

empty, ice-cold building to the little guest room. I felt as if I was walking through an ice mine in which no life could breathe, at any rate no warm-blooded human life. Only purified souls can endure it, the heroic souls who walk upon the glaciers of the spirit as in a garden of Paradise. They can be happy in it, for they know that God is near.

Everywhere I heard a rushing sound, a soft, incessant rushing as of water, which made the silence even more real to me.

"What is that strange rushing sound?" I asked.

"It is water," answered the Brother with a smile, as he stood still and held the lamp high up. "We have to let all the water taps in the monastery run day and night on account of the frost."

"It is the living water of which Jesus spoke," I thought, foolishly enough, in a sudden transport of feeling, and the crushing oppression caused by the terrifying strangeness of the silence changed in a flash to a sense of happiness.

In the small white room, with Saint Bruno for its protector, which I was to occupy during my stay in this monastery, the Brother showed me how to light the little Carthusian stove with wood shavings, and to feed the fire with the logs lying in a piled-up heap on the low chest at the foot of the bed. The fire fairly roared, and it became warm in the small white chamber.

We had supper at seven o'clock. This was later than

usual; at that hour the monks had already retired to rest. But before we began our meal one of the Fathers came to make us welcome.

With a little lantern in his hand he stood before me, dressed in his cream-colored habit with its great cowl and the heavy scapular held together at about waist level on either side by a loose broad band. There was a narrow crown about his shaven head, a thin circlet of hair.

He began to speak to us at once about the Carthusian way of life, as if he were resuming a conversation.

There we sat beside the little stove, three human beings in a silent world. There was a lamp on the table behind us. As I listened, I looked at him: he was still young, his face was severe yet possessed a tranquillity and goodness that were most impressive. The simple things he said about this intense life of the monastery came to me as a revelation. There was nothing in it but love, heroic love.

After supper we once more crossed the bare white corridors and passed through the tremendous silence, with the rushing of living water singing all round us as though it came from hidden springs. And now I was alone, back again in my little white room, where the only furnishings were a couple of chairs, a small wash-stand, a *prie-dieu*, a bed, the supply of wood, the table with the oil lamp on it, and the little stove.

Of course, I went to the window and stood there. It was night. Windless space. Glimmering white roofs—

or are they snow-clad hills?—all round the courtyard upon which my window opened. Above them, a violet-blue heaven decked with all the stars and the star-stuff of the Milky Way. And silence, the deep, deep silence of God and His universe. This was the silence which was certainty.

Inside, in the heart of the monastery—this crystal city in the mountains—the cloistered monks dwelled in their cell community. I knew this rich silence, for I remembered the days that I had spent in the Benedictine Abbey of Oosterhout. The silence here, like the silence there, was a tremendous, living presence, the biding place of the ineffable realities of the spirit.

How far, how immeasurably far, was this living silence from the disordered and inane happenings of what we call "a full and active life." Again and again, and more intensely than ever, it was borne in upon me that this was the place where man really answered to his own and his Creator's purpose—this place and a few others like it, cities of God here upon earth. If from here one could bring back to the world something of the life of these monks, however little it might be, even were it only an impotent longing for the Beautiful, the Sublime, the Simple, it would be a treasure for all eternity, the one lost coin for which I would sweep clean the house of my whole life.

THE DESERT FATHERS

IT was at Léon Bloy's that I gained for the first time a real understanding and a vivid picture of what the life of the Desert Fathers actually was in the early centuries of the Christian era.

I had, of course, heard and read from time to time of men and women who had snapped every tangible link with the world and withdrawn into solitary desert places. Who does not know of Saint Anthony, abbot and hermit, be it only from Flaubert's *Temptation of St. Anthony*? Nevertheless, those mighty figures had no direct reality for me; they were not alive. They were phantoms, fantastic ghosts, without form or content. In my mind they stood for romantic, legendary figures to whom we twentieth-century people could hardly be expected to pay any serious attention.

It was the good custom at Léon Bloy's in those days for one of the guests after the midday meal to read aloud a chapter out of a book about the saints, the others drinking their cup of coffee and smoking their cigarette as they listened.

And so every time we were all together at Bloy's home, and during the summer when we shared a house somewhere in the country, we read to one another regularly every day, out of a thick old book, the well-nigh miraculous lives of the first Desert Fathers. Then it was that these people came to life for me, with all their simple majesty and the direct immediacy of their love for God. Then it was that I learned to understand the high purpose of the solitude in which they lived alone with God, bringing at the same time into operation by the living prayer of their souls the mysterious reality of the Communion of Saints. These wonderful stories were told in the old book as simply as if they were about the most everyday things; and indeed the adventures of the spirit are intensely simple, but their scene is laid in the interior world. God was the only stake for which these players played, always and exclusively God. The spirit and love, this was reality, the precious stone they sought to possess by selling everything, abandoning everything, joyfully stripping themselves of everything, so as not to be encumbered as they raced toward the blinding goal. All the things that to the mass of people give life its value, all pleasures and enjoyments, all emotional rapture, riches, art, honor, power, the love of the senses and warm, human happiness, meant to them less than nothing.

For they saw God, and through the eyes of the spirit they perceived His creation, perfect in equilibrium and stupendous in the beauty of its ordering. The mystical rapture that possessed them brought with it the peace of reality. Their hearts burned within them. It was not that imagination had borne them away in an empty dream; they did not gaze into themselves. Their whole being had become simple and childlike in its gladness, and they were filled with a burning strength. Their silence, the silence of the contemplative, was no absence of activity, no little, mean-spirited, narrow easefulness, but a soundless traveling, at ever increasing speed, toward God.

It was a wonderful moment in the history of mankind when thousands, as in a second Exodus, entered the desert and its solitude and went to live in God's silence, while the world continued its furious round, suffocating beneath its pomp and drugged with the rotting splendor of pagandom in the false grandeur of its decline. And deep within it, unsullied, firm and pure, the strong kernel of Christianity was growing. The Roman emperors visited it with persecution after persecution. They cast it down but could neither split it up nor break it, that strange power which drew fresh strength from every crushing blow. Out of reach in the solitudes lived the monks and hermits, and they, the confessors of the Faith, together with the martyrs reaped down by the persecutions, preserved the living spirit in its purity.

By the Edict of Milan in 313, freedom of faith was proclaimed throughout the Roman Empire by Constantine the Great. Possessions were restored to Chris-

SAINT BRUNO

THE CLOISTER

tians from whom everything had previously been taken away. In 321, the Emperor instituted the observance of Sunday. In 323, he summoned the Council of Nicaea. Without any act of violence, but simply by the gentle, irresistible might of the spirit of love, Christianity won its place. Great was the enthusiasm of the Christians, who no longer needed to flee, but came out of the catacombs into the daylight to see Christianity acknowledged by the world.

But in this very acknowledgment there lurked a grave danger to the purity of their spirit. They were no longer rigorously segregated, and renewed contact with the world dimmed the singlehearted longing of the Christians. "Do not take on the ways of the world." And, as always in the Church, those whose love burned warmest, that is the simple and pure of heart, obeyed these words and the deep hunger of their own hearts, and set up a strong barrier between themselves and the world.

It is certain that large numbers of virgins were already living a life of celibacy in their own homes, and gathering for prayer at the third, sixth, and ninth hours, in memory of the judgment, crucifixion and death of Jesus. They rose up in the night in remembrance of the Resurrection. Already communities of religious women existed. Saint Anthony Abbot took his sister to such a cloister in the year 270, before he himself became a hermit.

Stronger and stronger grew the impulse to give up

the glamor of the world for the reality of life with God. For many, this urge reached the point where it became an irresistible force. At first men and women settled in huts and caves just outside the towns and villages. But their solitude was too often broken. Visitors disturbed them with admonitions and senseless sympathy, expressed pity for them, and asked them why they led such poverty-stricken lives when it was not only enjoyable but also perfectly permissible to live pleasantly in seemly prosperity and to enjoy all God's gifts. It was then the ascetics began to retreat deeper into the solitude.

There was hunger in their souls for the Absolute. Again and again at the great turning points of history, when chaos reigns and an outworn world is rushing to its death in the wildness of despair, this hunger has laid hold of numberless souls, with a need too sharp to be denied. There was the richness of joy in those souls too, and noble generosity, and simplicity, singlehearted simplicity. Thousands turned away from the pagan world, now sinking to its decline in a glitter of false magnificence. Without regret they flung it all away, and went back to the world they had left, for they were impelled by a singlehearted, boundless longing to live the tranquil life of the spirit. They migrated into the wilderness, to live within that silence which was, to their meditating hearts, brimful of God. And God never allows Himself to be outdone in the contest of sacrificing love.

The world was as empty then as it is in our day.
There was the insane and morbid spectacle of a civilization in the process of disintegration. It was phospho-
rescent matter, emptiness and demoniac show. Presently
the barbarians came and trampled underfoot the once
glorious Empire.

The Spirit keeps His house in solitude. He is an invisible, purifying fire. He is flame and darkness. Men,
heroes for love's sake, migrated into the wilderness to
be alone with God, even as a lover desires to be alone
with his beloved.

The hermits by the thousands settled in Palestine,
in Syria, in Mesopotamia, and in Egypt. This deep inner
life had already commenced with Saint Anthony and
his disciples, who populated the solitude of Pispir,
dwelling in cells, huts, and caves. Still deeper in the
solitude Saint Paul the Hermit dwelled in a grotto beside a tree; his clothing was its leaves and its fruit his
nourishment. Soon they formed themselves into settle-
ments of anchorites, such as the one founded by Ammon in the grim wilderness of Nitria, which Palladius,
the Greek bishop of Helenopolis in Bithynia, who
visited all these marvelous regions, describes in his
Lausiac History, written about 420 in Greek for
Lausus, chamberlain of Theodosius II.

There in Nitria dwelt five thousand of them, scat-
tered over the mountain in huts, either separately or
in twos and threes. All worked for the community, as

gardeners, bakers, carpenters, or as cooks in the great kitchen. Anyone was charitably received in the guest quarters. A stranger might stay as long as he would, but after a week he had to work with the Brothers. There were seven bakehouses for bread. The church stood in the middle of the settlement, and there the anchorites gathered on Saturdays and Sundays for Mass and the offices, which were carried on by eight priests. On the other days a bell was rung in the silence of the wilderness at the hours of prayer. Then might be heard a soft, far-away singing of psalms from the thousands of cells, as though Thy Kingdom had come and in that place earth had become Paradise. At those prayer hours the anchorite rediscovered the sweet, wordless intercourse which was the daily bread of the first man and woman. He would shut his house, and say to his soul, "Never again descend from Heaven. There thou hast the Angels and Archangels, the Powers and Dominions, the Thrones and Principalities, the Cherubim and Seraphim, Mary their Queen and our Mother, and the Holy, Holy, Holy God of the Universe. Come thou not lower than the heavens. . . ." And God spoke and listened to Himself in that soul.

They were great pioneers. One should read the lives of these simple souls, these heroes unconscious of their own heroism, who did not seek themselves but in utter simplicity listened to God and whispered with their guardian angels—we may learn of them in the entranc-

ing stories of Ammon, Macarius, Melania, Piteroem, of
Thaïs and Serapion, of Abraham and his niece, of
Simeon Stylites, and of many, many others. In this way
one may receive into one's heart something, if only a
reflection, of the light of these humble lives absorbed in
God.

Legends! Legends! Sublime legends, if you like—I
hear them saying it, the people who have something
better to do than to waste their precious time on such
extravagant dreams. Besides, they say, there may pos-
sibly have been such creatures in those days, but not
nowadays. It is too childish an idea for these days of
mental hygiene and films, of airplanes and exact sci-
ences, of psychoanalysis and astronomical calculations.

And yet all these are things that do not touch the
soul at all. A soul that knows God is far less moved by
these trifles than the farthest star in the most distant
solar system would be affected if, at some point during
the millions of light years of its development, a new
continent should emerge from the Pacific Ocean. God
calls, and the soul rushes to meet Him. It leaves everything and, as the blind world fittingly puts it, "buries
itself in a monastery." It becomes a living soul.

It has always been so, and it happens today just as it
did in those first centuries, when the human voice of
Jesus still echoed more clearly in the hearts of men
and it had only recently come to pass that a God was
nailed to a cross. Even today, every *living* soul has

been there, and has seen it, and has gazed into the failing eyes of Him who for love's sake suffered Himself to fail.

Even such a living soul was Saint Bruno, the founder of the Carthusians. Like a Desert Father he sought the barren solitude of the mountaintops after having worked for years in the world where he had become famous for his learning—his faith ever wedded to sound dogma, his love rich in good works. Far off, in the Alps of Dauphiné, he set up his dwelling with a few of his brothers. He forced his way into the inhospitable, unyielding wilderness with the low cry, *O Bonitas!* ever upon his lips.

Like all founders of contemplative orders in the West, he took the rule of Saint Benedict, Patriarch of the Occident, as the guiding principle of life for himself and his brethren, but he added, from the life of the Desert Fathers, the personal solitude, the strict fasting, and the great silence. He put together the ideals of the hermitage and the cloistered community, and welded them into a whole in the Carthusian Order.

And there, where he first lived with his hermit monks, inaccessibly far from the world, in deepest seclusion amid the silence of mountain and wood, practicing no activity as the world understands that word but achieving the mighty deed of contemplating God and praying without ceasing, choosing the contemplative life which Jesus called "the better part"—

there, in that very place, arose soon afterward the mother house of the Carthusian Order, which has been renowned ever since his time, the holy capital of all Charterhouses. It is called the Grande Chartreuse, the Great Charterhouse, as one speaks of Charlemagne, Charles the Great.

3

SAINT BRUNO

THE wisdom, judgment, and convictions of wordly people consist largely, if not entirely, of secondhand opinions and a countless number of dull and inane commonplaces unblushingly flung together. With regard to the monastic life such people cherish a fixed idea in whose defense they would gleefully be led to torture, for their stupidity is as impervious as reinforced concrete. Their idea is that men and women, of whatever age and education, who "take refuge" in a cloister, and more especially in the enclosed monasteries of the contemplatives, are really misfits, individuals who could never have counted for much in the active life of the world—the phrase "to count for much" having reference, of course, to a good social position, earning a lot of money, making one's way in life, a brilliant marriage, becoming a pillar of society, etc.—that these men and women are without vitality or will power, without daring or the courage to face life, without personality, without initiative, without character, without talent; in short, helpless, self-centered weaklings with a touch of sugary sentimentality in their nature and the leaning toward a gloomy, exaggerated kind of piety.

There could be no more foolish judgment. Moreover the facts give it the lie.

I once heard an abbot say, "As novices for our monastery I can make use only of the best young men the world has to offer, the elite of heart and soul. And that is not enough: they must have something more besides."

These young men have grasped the true proportion of things: everything that is valuable to one who feels at home in a materialistic world means less than nothing to them. Real monks are no weak-kneed shirkers fleeing to the solitude and silence of a monastery out of fear of life or dislike of mankind, out of weariness and a shrinking longing—there are the battlefields of the spirit!—for a life peaceful and free from daily annoyances and carking cares and miseries.

The passion that has been spurring them on springs from a very different source. It seeks its outlet in the steep, straight way to God, solely and purely for love of God and love of man. To them the word "love" is neither a hollow sound nor a lovely, meaningless syllable with pleasant emotional associations; it is reality; it is the stuff of their being; it lives, breathes, moves, thinks, and speaks with them and in them. It has become the sight of their eyes and the pulse of their heart. Yes, it is true: these men and women no longer have a place in our social system. They are too pure and high for the stagnant pool in which we live. But if there is any purity left in the world, if there is any hungering and thirsting after the Sublime, if there are a few who strive to bring a little love, real love, into men's lives and to purify a little the air of human society, we have these quiet contemplatives to thank for it. For it is in their cloisters, at those invisible but actual hearths where the fires of charity burn bright, that our longing and our strong desires receive the fuel that keeps them alive.

And these are the poor, world-weary misfits! What of Benedict, Bruno, Francis, Dominic, Ignatius?—to confine ourselves to the founders of the great orders. Surely it cannot be doubted that they would have counted for much in the world as leaders of men. And think of such a woman as Teresa. No, they had all seen the straight road to their goal, and that is why they turned away from the world: they did not want to lose any time.

Bruno's life story makes it crystal clear that he was not a man driven by shyness of his fellows, or by the disillusionment caused by failure, to bury himself in solitude far from the daily strife, a deserter fleeing before the army of worldly cares. Imagine the inhospitable nature of the barren Alpine range of Dauphiné, with its dark, untrodden fir woods, its yawning chasms and perpendicular rocky precipices and the incessant

chatter of rushing streams, way back in the eleventh
century when there were neither roads nor Alpine clubs
nor Cook's tours nor those other associations for the
promotion of the tourist traffic which so sadly invade
the beauties of nature. Bruno's ascent to that solitude
was the strongest action in a life rich in action.

He had not from the beginning seen the direction his
life was to take. Yet the years of his active life were a
compelling preparation for his later call, because he
paid unwavering attention to what God showed him,
and allowed himself to be led. He was born around
1035 at Cologne, of the noble and ancient family of
Hartenfaust, and, being called to the priesthood from
his earliest days, he attended the school of Saint Cuni-
bert in his native city. His clear understanding and
deep, simple piety aroused admiration and great ex-
pectations. But he shunned the enthusiastic apprecia-
tion of his fellow townsmen and feared the honor they
paid him, as indeed he feared even his happy family life
with parents and relatives. He moved to France and
there continued his studies as a foreign student at the
cathedral school of Reims. He was seeking obscurity,
not such honor and fame as the world would give
him. After his ordination as a priest, Bruno traveled all
over the country, a stranger and nameless, preaching
the Gospel and receiving none of the honor due to his
name and learning, known only for his love of souls.

He thought he had found his lifework: to preach to
the people and rouse in simple hearts the love of Jesus.

Deprivations, dangers, and solitude were the faithful companions of his apostolic labors.

The gifted and learned young man, whose eloquence had thrown the literati of Reims and Cologne into ecstasies (he seems also to have taught at the University of Paris) had become an ordinary priest, whose love enabled him to find words simple enough to touch the hard hearts of the people. But the Archbishop of Reims, Saint Gervais, recalled him and appointed him chancellor of the schools of the diocese. This task of headmaster and director he carried out perfectly. They called him not simply "Master," but "Father." He was a great scholar, but he remained too the simple, gentle, wise priest. One of his pupils was afterward Pope Urban II. Bruno shaped souls both strong and great.

Yet life in the world was a trial and a burden to him. Hunger and thirst after perfection drove him toward that deep life alone with God which is achieved by the fully cloistered monk in his divine solitude.

Then the holy Archbishop of Reims died. Manasses, the usurper, succeeded him, and none could stand against the cunning violence of this conscienceless prelate. Only Bruno stood firm, in quiet, inexorable strength. To yield or give way were unthinkable to him, and, with the same calm with which he had received the adulation of other days, he now stood immovable amid savage attacks and grim confusion: for he was leaning upon God. And yet, these things caused him bitter grief, not for himself—his soul had its dwelling elsewhere—but because of infamy brought upon the Church. Rome sent a papal legate; a council met at Autun; Manasses was removed. And it should cause no surprise that Bruno was picked out as the one and only man capable of taking upon himself the glorious but onerous office of Bishop of Reims.

But it was not his work. He fled. It had become clear to him what God would have of him. Even when he was a teacher at the cathedral school and later as chancellor, he had felt the need of retiring frequently to a little, quiet garden, cut off from noise and clamor, and there he would consort with two friends, and talk with them earnestly and persuasively, in passionate, burning words, about the cloistered life of which he dreamed. To them he revealed his hidden longing for perfect solitude alone with God. But these two priests, Fulcius and Raoul, were never more to him than his first hearers. Everyone has his own task and vocation; and to them it seemed impossibly difficult to cast the world away entirely, simply to turn one's back upon it and choose the better part. Others listened to him and understood his love, his unfathomable love. "One seemed to be hearing God Himself," says a chronicler who describes Bruno's eloquence in sublimely naïve words. But Bruno was a humble man. What did he know of the monastic life? He had still to learn.

He went to Molesme, where the abbot was that Robert who afterward became the founder of the Cistercians. Yet to him it seemed that even the strict life there did not go far enough. He dreamed of the wilderness, of solitude and deep silence, of contemplation, of being absorbed into God. His pattern was the life of the hermits of early Christendom, who lived in inaccessible places in Egypt, Syria, Mesopotamia, and Palestine. He talked his plans over with Robert. Together they sought a place where Bruno could establish himself with his six companions: four priests, Landuin, Stephen of Bourg, Stephen of Die and the chaplain Hugo; and two laymen, Andrew and Guerin. And they decided upon the Alps of Dauphiné which they knew only by name.

The final decision was made and the day of departure fixed. The evening before, Bruno talked to his companions about the difficult, comfortless life that awaited them. They laughed at the thought; there was no hesitation in their hearts; they were going with him. Bruno spent the whole night in prayer in the abbey church of Molesme, deep hours, of immeasurable value for the Church and for all mankind. And a strange tremor passed through the watchful, listening angel bands. Bruno in his vision saw three angels who announced to him that God was with him and would guide him.

They left, forsaking those apostolic labors which are limited to separate districts with visible boundaries, in favor of the mission work whose parish is the whole wide world. For all mankind in all the world becomes the mission parish of the contemplative monk. From his cell, and from the unshakable contemplation of God, he guards and guides through the night of faith the invisible flocks of souls especially entrusted to him, for whose welfare he is responsible, just as on Christmas Night the shepherds led their sheep to the Stable at Bethlehem.

On Saint John's Day in 1084, Bruno and his six companions came to Bishop Hugh at Grenoble. This bishop had followed the lectures of the saintly teacher at Reims. He had been informed of their coming in a dream in which he had been transported to the wildest part of the mountain range and set down in the midst of woods where the voices of falling avalanches echoed about him. Suddenly he had seen a lovely church rise up in that place, and on its highest pinnacle there had rested seven glittering stars.

Bishop Hugh described the place to them. It was an uninhabitable district among the mountain peaks, to which no man had yet penetrated. Because of the severity of the climate, it was even more completely avoided by men than the solitary parts of the Egyptian wilderness. But while the Bishop was speaking, Bruno's joy became exultation: this spot, terrifying in its grandeur, was the blessed land for which he had longed as a man longs for home. They set out to reach it. It was a slow journey. There were no roads, not even footpaths. But Bishop Hugh and the angels showed them the appointed way. They climbed gradually higher and higher. The air was pure as the air of Paradise. Like seekers for gold, they traveled steadfastly onward, these heavenly adventurers, sense and soul possessed with a happy longing. Without reckoning of danger, they climbed down into the dim depths of an abyss, then up the other side into the light once more. With their axes they cut themselves a path through the mighty mountain forests. It was as if nature, like an army of demons, took arms against these invaders, who believed, in their childlike way, that they could storm the Kingdom of Heaven by the force of their love. Little by little they made their way deeper and deeper into the dread, solitary wilderness. At last they reached the spot seen by Bishop Hugh in his dream, a place awful in its desolation and preternatural silence, among gigantic masses of rock which had been hurled there ages ago by volcanoes long extinct. The seven hermits had reached their goal, and they began their work; they built huts from branches, and a wooden chapel dedicated to the Mother of God, Our Lady of Casalibus.

Bishop Hugh went back to Grenoble, but he did not forget the monks. He became their protector, providing for their needs, and seeing that nothing disturbed the silence of their life and the gentle vehemence of their mighty act of prayer. He knew the value of it. He knew that the moving and controlling power of the spiritual cosmos is the prayer of contemplatives who fulfill the purpose of creation by living wholly and only for God, and through God for men. They are the most necessary of all. "Seek ye first the kingdom of

THE CHARTERHOUSE OF LA VALSAINTE

ENTRANCE TO THE CHAPEL

God and his justice, and all these things shall be added unto you."

Bruno loved his solitude. Even as his father Benedict, he reposed in the tremendous, brimming silence of the spirit. He was an abyss into which the Niagara of Love Divine cast itself down. He gathered light from beyond the world and sent it forth again in shining rays upon its way. He did not seek to accomplish great deeds nor to exercise any visible influence. His silence was broken only now and again by the cry: *O Bonitas!* which rose from the depth of his heart. Bruno believed that he was buried alive in the solitude of the wild mountain woods; he thought that the world had forgotten him. But the world knew of him.

It was a cruel surprise for Bruno when Pope Urban II summoned him to Rome to be his counselor and wise helper in the government of the Church and in the bitter strife against evil. He made the sacrifice, obeyed and went, nevermore to see the little settlement he had founded, which was destined to grow and one day become that mighty marvel, the Grande Chartreuse, mother house of a great order.

Before his departure Bruno appointed Landuin as his successor. It was a heavy trial for them all. Bruno was anxious and afraid: he had a presentiment of the future that amounted almost to a vision. The six monks stayed behind in orphaned loneliness. Their father had gone away, he who had inspired them and by his goodness and shining example had made them rise far above themselves. They were sheep without their shepherd. Without Bruno, the solitude was nearly too much for them. At last they could bear it no longer: they must see their father Bruno once more; they must leave the huts and the chapel in the mountains and go, all together, to him in Rome.

Bruno received them without reproaching them for their weakness, however deep his own grief may have been. He even sought a place for them in Rome, where they might resume their interrupted cloistered life. And this he did with the full consent of the Pope, who ever looked to the enclosed orders for the sanctity that would redeem the times and, with a deep insight into the power of the contemplative life, encouraged new foundations.

At first it looked as though Bruno's arrangements for them would be successful: the building which had once been the Baths of Diocletian was appointed their dwelling place. But in the middle of the city like this their solitude was too much disturbed by friends and admirers, as well as by prying persons and enemies. Moreover, Bruno himself was overwhelmed with work, and came but seldom to his brothers. But when he did come, he spoke to them about the life of a truly cloistered monk, and the six monks looked into their consciences and repented of their cowardice. They grew homesick for their huts and mountain heights, and asked leave to return to the Chartreuse, even without their father Bruno, for he must stay in Rome. So, purified by their trials, their zeal burning brighter than ever before, and enriched in numbers—for new brothers had joined them since their flight—they carried out the return journey and took up once more the magnificent silent work of praying monks. Since that time the sublime life in that solitary place among the mountains of Dauphiné has never been interrupted except once by the violence of the French Revolution and again by the crass stupidity of the persecution and expropriation of 1903.

Some years later, Bruno obtained permission from Pope Urban to leave Rome, but he was destined never to return to the Grande Chartreuse. The inhabitants of Reggio Calabria asked the Pope to give them Bruno as their archbishop. The Pope consented, but Bruno was longing for solitude as a child longs for its mother, and he managed, by the holy importunity of his pleading, to move the Pope to permit his withdrawal from the world, this time for good.

With a few followers Bruno established himself in Calabria, in a wild, solitary place in the diocese of Squillace, in the forsaken region of Torra. Thus he founded the second Charterhouse, and there he died in 1101, having outlived his six beloved companions. Probably he never fully realized that by restoring, under God, the heroic way of life of the Desert Fathers he had founded that enclosed order which ranks highest in the spiritual hierarchy, the order of the Carthusians.

4

DAYS AND NIGHTS IN THE CHARTERHOUSE OF LA VALSAINTE

IT was half-past six in the morning of December 24th, and dark in the ice-cold corridors. Outside the moon was shining upon windowpanes made opaque by the frost. Around us silence breathed like a wind from the pole, the inexpressible presence of the very essence of silence, everywhere, within and without.

We had left our warm little rooms and come to the Brothers' chapel, where a single candle was burning upon the altar, a friendly signal light. A tall, silent white monk, whom I recognized, was there, making preparations for the celebration of Mass. Then the priest monk came in, the one who had been with us the evening before. He was to say Mass for us. After a short prayer on the altar steps, the two monks, standing, said the morning Office of Our Lady. Their voices sounded soft but clear in the immeasurable silence.

The priest put on the vestments. He poured the wine into the chalice. The Carthusian Mass began.

The priest stood on the Gospel side at the foot of the altar, with his left side toward the altar. Opposite him, on the Epistle side, stood the young monk who was serving. And in full tones they repeated alternately the wonderful dialogue at the beginning of the Mass:

In Nomine Patris et Filii et Spiritus Sancti. Amen.

P. *Pone, Domine, custodiam ori meo.*

R. *Et ostium circumstantiae labiis meis.*

P. *Confiteor Deo et beatae Mariae et omnibus Sanctis et vobis, fratres, quia peccavi nimis, mea culpa per superbiam, cogitatione, locutione et omissione, precor vos orate pro me.*

R. *Misereatur tui omnipotens Deus, per intercessionem beatae Mariae et omnium Sanctorum, et dimittat tibi omnia peccata tua et perducat te ad vitam aeternam.*

[In the name of the Father and of the Son and of the Holy Ghost, Amen.

P. Set a watch, O Lord, before my mouth.

R. And a door round about my lips.

P. I confess to God and to the Blessed Virgin and to all the Saints and to you, brethren, because I have sinned exceedingly, through my fault out of pride, in thought, in speech and in omission, I beg you pray for me.

R. May Almighty God have mercy on you, through the intercession of Blessed Mary and of all the Saints, and may He forgive all your sins and lead you to life everlasting.]

After the server had said the *Confiteor*, the priest ascended to the altar. The Mass proceeded, to the accompaniment of movements Eastern in rhythm and expressive of ecstasy. When the water was mingled with the wine, the priest prayed: *De latere Domini Nostri Jesu Christi exivit sanguis et aqua in remissionem peccatorum. In Nomine Patris et Filii et Spiritus Sancti. Amen.* [From the side of Our Lord Jesus Christ blood and water poured forth for the remission of sins. In the name of the Father and of the Son and of the Holy Ghost. Amen.]

After the consecration only the sacred Host was elevated, not the chalice with the Precious Blood. There is no blessing after the Mass, nor is the Gospel of Saint John read at the end. Thus was Mass celebrated in the diocese of Lyons in the eleventh century, when Saint Bruno was on earth.

The two monks said the thanksgiving prayers, stretched out on the floor on their right and left side respectively, their knees a little drawn up, their weight upon an elbow which rested upon the scapular spread out in front of them. Dawn lingered pale and icy cold against the dim windowpanes.

Here there must be a spiritual fire that consumes everything. "God is an all-consuming fire."

The monks knew that fire.

We went away in silence. In a little while, at 10 o'clock, the High Mass of Christmas Eve would be sung by the whole monastery.

Day broke as we were breakfasting in the little guest refectory at 8 o'clock. There was as yet no sun. It was still hidden behind the mountain which encloses the valley on the east. While we were walking through deep, dry snow in the garden behind the cells of the Carthusians, the glow above the sharply defined mountaintop grew brighter and brighter. The silence in this white world was perfect. Everything was white: the roofs were white; the mountains were white in their soft, smooth, spotless cloaks of snow. The only dark flecks were the woods on the lower slopes, and the tremendous, naked rock-faces which rise sheer above. Now the white was mingled with gold as suddenly, over the tender white of the mountain barrier, sunlight streamed into the valley from the cold, cloudless sky. The flower of day had opened; light had come to the world as grace enters into a soul.

I only gazed and listened. There was nothing but silence around me, a profound silence that lived and breathed; it was within me, too, penetrating to the profoundest depth of my heart, a nameless presence.

On the north the valley was bounded by a wide mountain amphitheater; on the right and on the left rose the silent white barriers of the mountains, and in front of me, to the southwest, there was the valley formed by the Javroz, which flowed at the bottom of a deep gorge beneath its covering of ice. Above the silent monastery and the monks' cells, out of a chimney here and there, blue smoke crept slowly up into the air in a straight line, like a burnt offering. Awful and almost unbearable was the loneliness of the monastery. It lay in this breath-taking solitude as though it had fallen down from heaven, a pure, shining crystal with polished facets.

I now knew the surroundings and the outward appearance of the monastery. Now we were going to penetrate to its very heart.

At 10 o'clock we sat in the gallery of the church. The church was lofty and narrow, and divided into two parts by a partition of dark wood broken by a door carved in an open design and connecting the choir of the Fathers with the space where the Brothers attend offices and Mass. This space is half roofed over by a gallery. From our places we overlooked the church and the distant altar.

The white monks came in one after another, bowed before the altar, pulled the bell rope one at a time, each placing it in the outstretched hand of the one behind him, and then going to their places in the choir stalls. Everything was marked by a stern, naked simplicity. The daily sung High Mass of the monastery is always celebrated by one priest alone; to this rule no exception is ever made. All the psalm singing was in strong, manly rhythm and rugged tone. The *Gloria Patri et Filio et*

Spiritui Sancto was long drawn out in a majestic way with slow, full notes. The monks sang the very oldest Gregorian chants, always without an organ, and in strong, powerful voices (*viva et rotunda voce*).

I was trembling both with the piercing, icy cold and with an emotion that overmastered and enveloped me. As I sat listening, I became lost to all else; my consciousness was quickened as though I had for the first time learned to know myself; my tense listening had become a wordless prayer.

Faith was no vague, far-off experience here, no pale dream to comfort weak, sensitive souls; it was reality. What Jesus said was here translated into unequivocal fact, into living acts of the soul, untouched by compromise or any of the reserves that spring from suppressed selfishness. Fully and generously they had interpreted Jesus' words: "Every one of you that doth not renounce all that he possesseth, cannot be my disciple."

Later in the day we went over the monastery. My companion knew the way, and we went together through the corridors, streets of an icebound city. Our footsteps rang clear in those strange, vaulted streets, which looked like long ice tunnels, so white and cold did they seem behind the window panes coated thick with frost. The cells of the monks open upon these corridors. Each dwelling place has above its door a letter of the alphabet and a text from Holy Scripture: "Our conversation is in heaven." We went through

those deep, empty tunnels, feeling as if they were ways
hollowed out through the glaciers of the spirit. Could
it be that there was sin in this place? Not our sort of
sin. Here the battle was for the height, and for the
height above the height. Here we were at an altitude
of 3,200 feet. One would have to climb still higher to
reach the silent, dangerous glaciers and higher still to
their very summits where valley folk could no longer
breathe, but where the spirit finds more abundant life.
Life here is white as lightning-fire. It looks pitiless and
mad, a reckless adventure. But it is pure tenderness and
fire; nothing but love. It is goodness. *O Bonitas!*

At the center of the monastery, in the enclosed garden surrounded by the cloisters, lies the graveyard,
with its black crosses standing erect in the snow. There
we said the *Magnificat*, and for ourselves the *De Pro-
fundis*. We were the dead. They were the living.

It is all so inexpressibly simple. Here life is made
whole by gentle force and utter goodness. What strug-
gles this must have cost, and what sufferings! For human nature sets itself against wholeness: there are so
many centrifugal forces at work in us. It is love alone
that constrains all that is in us to be at one; the fire of
love consumes all else. "God is an all-consuming fire."

We were allowed to go into the refectory of the
Fathers and the refectory of the Brothers. There they
have their meals together in silence on Sundays and on

feast days. Elsewhere in this cold little city there is a chapel in which is stored a wondrous treasure—the relics of hundreds of saints. We went into the chapel of the novitiate, too, where the novice master says Mass daily for his novices, and instructs them in the Carthusian way of life, whose sole aim is to be alone with God: *Soli Deo*. These words appear outside the monastery church, above the entrance to the first court-yard. Then we also visited an uninhabited cell. I wanted to realize the way of this life, to comprehend something of its daily reality and mystery. Therefore I was permitted, in addition, to visit the cell of a monk whom I had known in the world, long—how long?—ago. He conversed with me, and spoke of deep and simple things.

As this monastery is built against the slope of the mountain, the arrangement of the cell dwellings differs a little from that in other Carthusian monasteries. From the cloisters one comes through the main door to the first floor of the cell dwelling. A bellpull hangs beside the door and there too is the deep window opening into which a Brother puts food, already prepared, for the solitary. All the food is prepared in the monastery kitchen.

One comes first into a wide passage with a wooden floor, where the monk can pace to and fro. He has plenty of room, as far as that goes: the whole cell is spacious and clear—and bare. To get into the cell proper, which is his living room, bedroom and place

of prayer, one passes through a smaller room in which
there stands a statue of Our Blessed Lady. Whenever
the Carthusian monk leaves his cell or comes back
home, he kneels and salutes the Holy Mother. And so
this apartment is known as the *Ave Maria*. There is
nothing in it but Our Lady's statue and a few flowers
—flowers which the monk has grown in his own little
garden. A connecting door affords an entrance into
the cell, which is a spacious, square room. In the thick
outer wall a window with a deep sill opens onto the
garden and, incidentally, upon the stark beauty of the
mountains.

In this room the Carthusian lives. Here the greater
part of his life is spent—thirty, forty, fifty, sixty, suc-
cessive years. On the side of the room opposite his one
window he has his oratory, a choir stall with shelves
and a wooden kneeler, a crucifix, and his prayer books.
Here, praying alone but with all the bodily movements
proper to community prayer in choir, he says the Office
of Our Lady and, on most days of the year, the Little
Hours. Mary encircles a Carthusian's day: at about
eleven every night he starts the fair arc of his day with
Matins from the Office of Our Lady, and at half-past
six in the evening, immediately before he sleeps, he
ends it with Compline from her office. But this is not
the only place in which he prays, for the monk's interior prayer goes on through the whole day, and
through all the days of his life.

Next to this prayer corner there is a sort of cupboard

bed without doors, shut off from the room by a green curtain. A couple of grey blankets lie folded on the hard straw mattress, for everything has its proper place. Here the monk sleeps from half-past six in the evening until eleven—though he may rise at ten o'clock or even earlier to sing the night office in the church—and again from two or three o'clock in the morning till six.

Beside the window, across the corner of the room, there stands a table of white wood at which the monk sits to read, study, or write, confining himself always, of course, to spiritual subjects. Against the wall behind him is a bookcase of white wood, containing books on asceticism and mysticism. If he desires other books, there is the great library of the monastery. Near the door, almost in the middle of the cell, stands the typical little Carthusian stove.

The wide window sill is the monk's dining room. In a drawer and in a little cupboard are his table napkin, his wooden spoon and fork, and an earthenware beaker with two handles. He fetches his meal from the small window opening beside the outer door and, sitting at his window, eats it in solitude. On feast days, however, and on Sundays, he goes at the same hour to the monks' refectory and takes his meals there with his brethren.

The monk has a loft, too, a storeroom for turf and other fuel, and two more rooms on the same level as the garden. In the first he cuts and saws great blocks of wood, making them the size and shape required for his little stove; and in the other, next door, he has a bench and a lathe. There, at fixed hours, he may work or amuse himself in any way he likes, carving figures in wood, making various objects, or carpentering to his heart's content.

And then he has his garden. This is enclosed on two sides by his own cell dwelling. On the third side it is bounded by his neighbor's blind wall. Along the fourth runs a fairly high wall above which the mountains are visible in the distance—but the Carthusian dwells upon other mountains.

I have never seen a Carthusian garden in the summer. When I was there the gardens were deep in snow. In spring and summer the dweller may grow as many flowers as he likes, and there are fruit trees of a very good quality trained along the walls.

Thus the daily life of the cloistered monk is extremely simple and clear. It has the bright purity of the air upon the mountaintops of the spirit. In every way this life is the diametric opposite of all those things which the world pursues, thinking thereby to make life worth living. It burns its way to God in a taut line of living fire; it outstrips all bounds, and is perfect in its equilibrium.

Wise moderation, the *discretio* of the father and founder of the order, and a profound knowledge of the human soul have laid it down that these solitaries must have some intercourse with one another. On this plane of life there are great dangers unknown to us. The contemplative life is the anteroom of Paradise, but it is also a battlefield beside which our wars are child's play. And it has the blessedness of peace, for there is naught in it but love.

On Sundays and feast days the monks may spend their recreation time together, and one day a week they go for a walk, three or four hours long, into the mountains outside the monastery—this is the *spatiamentum*. Then they talk and are like happy children of God. "Rejoice in the Lord always; again, I say, rejoice."

The solitude, the refraining from speech, the night choir and the daily sung High Mass, the study and the recreation, the community meals on Sundays and feast days in the common refectory, the reining in of natural instincts, the walking and talking, and the silence again, every function of life, every act, every moment of sitting still, every gesture, every posture, every breath of the spirit and of the heart, and the quiet of this great solitude, everything in this way of life so strictly yet so gently ordered, everything always has one and one goal only—the closest possible union with God, to live heart to heart with God in the utter self-giving of love.

It was Christmas Eve. In the pitiless, freezing night-cold we sat again in the gallery up above the dimly lighted church. Outside, a wonderful, starry heaven spread above a white world. The monks had come out of their cells, and now, cowl drawn over head and small lighted lantern in their hands, they passed in silence along the ice tunnels to their work, the work of God

—God's white mineworkers, each with his invisible companion, his guardian angel, at his side. At a quarter to ten they had already been called by the monastery bell and were all standing at the mine-head in their mountain gully, the choir.

Silence and solitude, oceans wide as the sky which even a Columbus could not cross, beleaguer them round about and cut off both them and us from the world's harlequinade. Outside this place everything was unreal. The focal point of life was here. There *is* nothing else anywhere on earth but this narrow space between high dark walls with the stark night all around, this little spot and some other houses like it, where life dwells and where men and women stand singing in the night, human beings raising their song in prayer to God.

We followed the singing, both the words and the neums, in a great office book that lay open before us on the wide balustrade in the ring of golden light cast by an oil lamp. All the antiphons, psalms, and responses were sung. I felt moved to my innermost being. On the stroke of twelve, Midnight Mass began.

Here there were none of the embellishments of the Christmas Feast, no ornaments, no pomp, except that a multitude of candles had been lighted, whole rows of them high up along the walls behind and on either side of the altar. The Vicar sang Mass, and he and the deacon alone communicated. No one else received Our Lord. Except for the three main Masses, the monks

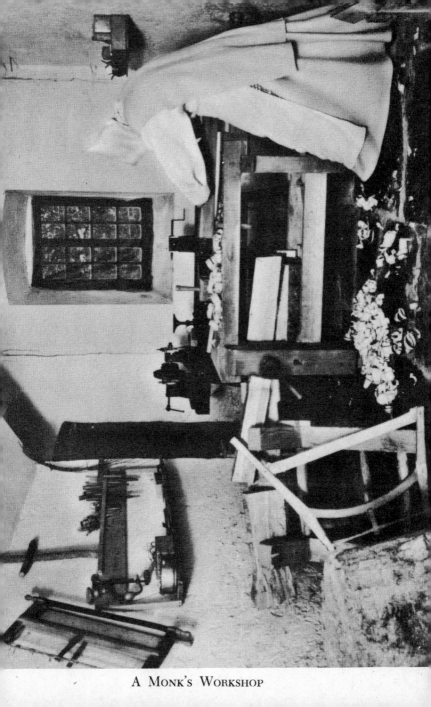

A Monk's Workshop

A Monk's Cell

who are priests do not say Mass on this day; neither do they all say Mass on Easter or Whitsunday. They receive Communion at the Morning Mass as do the juniors and the novices. We two guests received the Body of Jesus with the Brothers at the Mass of Dawn, kneeling in a wide circle before the altar, with a long, white communion cloth spread over our hands.

Here Christmas is celebrated in the pure cold of the spirit, but it is a burning cold. So great it is and wide, so hard has solitude frozen it, that we remain hidden for hours and hours in the warm Heart of Love.

The Carthusian Christmas is a naked feast. All that happens takes place at a terrifying height, between the soul and God. There is but one mountain path that leads, sheer and straight, up to the lonely glaciers of this angelic life: it is the life of pure contemplation.

5

THE CARTHUSIANS
AND OURSELVES

LIFE in the world has become unbalanced, and most of us do not know it. The pattern has been lost, and we do not want to admit it. We hold as valuable, as essentially important and uniquely interesting, things that are really worthless, senseless, impure, or sordid. In plain language, everything is upside down. No longer is anything too holy to be touched. A young man—no barbarian: barbarians are not so cynical and brainy—once said, with contemptuous pity, of one of his companions, that he had not yet "taken Christianity apart," as he himself had done. We enjoy being complicated, and cherish our sordid, restless thoughts. We do not want simplicity and silence. We do not want purity and the consuming fire of love.

A whole generation, not only of writers but of innocent men and women, has been ruined by a smattering of psychological knowledge; it considers itself far more advanced than the repentant sinner with his clear self-knowledge. Men of letters empty out the bear pits of their subconscious mind over the heads of voracious readers, who are delighted by their subtle, cleverly worded revelations of those things which lie in the darkness at the bottom of every human soul.

Nowadays we say, "Life! this is life!" and we are sure that our minds are enriched by a deeper insight into the nature of that sordid darkness. We do not see the defilement. We choose this insight into chaos rather than order, peace, and the hunger and thirst after God. No longer do we utter the command: "Be-gone, Satan!" No longer do we pray, strong in our helplessness: "Saint Michael, the archangel, defend us in battle; be our protection against the malice and snares of the devil. . . ." We wade through the slime, un-aware that Evil himself is our companion.

What then can the life of these solitaries mean to us who feel we are superior to them in our knowledge of life—even those of us who are believers and who think we are doing all we should? We rush aimlessly about; we have subdued the forces of nature and mecha-nized life to the highest degree; like men possessed, we chase a will-o'-the-wisp through our own hearts and across the earth's surface. We cannot see beyond this short life. To us it is a lightning flash of consciousness, enduring but a moment between two endless nights. And, from this moment, as from a fruit filled with poisonous juice, we wish to squeeze out every drop and to enjoy it to the smallest fraction of a second.

And faith, the strong, living faith that builds a bridge for the spirit between time and eternity, leading on to the pure, eternal Light of God—where shall we still find that faith?

Yet, there are some people—I do not mean those whose eyes are unopened to the tragic unrest about them and who live more like contented animals—but those others whose souls within them, like a clear, bright day, are in perfect equilibrium; the high, silent ones who know peace. Upon their tranquil hearts the arms of the Cross are balanced, burdened with all the sufferings and martyrdoms of their brother men. Their home is in the abyss of Light. A few such souls are to be found, here and there in the world, but there are far more of them in the abodes of silence, in the monasteries of the contemplative orders.

When one has been in such a monastery, Benedictine, Trappist, or Carthusian, and has gained some idea, however imperfect, of that life whose light is other than that in which we worldlings walk, then one knows for evermore that, in its deep passion and swift course toward mankind's Goal, such a life follows the curve of a sublime pattern. I know that it is a cheap and obvious commonplace to point to the contrast between that pregnant silence, that meek yearning after God, and our self-important bluster, our frantic busyness, our chatter and our equivocations. But it is forced irresistibly upon one's mind.

The men and women in convents live calmly and

silently. They deny themselves, while we look for ease and comfort; they have eyes as clear as water and a restful posture of body, while our faces bear the marks of all our sins, and we race about all our days. We do not understand silence; we think that it is emptiness. And it is in reality the fullness of abundance. We look upon those rare souls who renounce the world as in some sort inferior, weaklings and cowards in the face of life. But it is they who are heroes, strong and great. And theirs is the real life.

Indeed there is no better thing that we could do than from time to time, and that as often as possible, to place ourselves in perfect silence within the circle which radiates from these glowing centers of life, and to strive, although we live amid the world's senseless tumult, to build a cell within our own hearts, a cloistered place to which we may retreat, and in silent rapture of heart and spirit listen to the powerful and tender murmur of divine Love.

The thought that there are monasteries where everything is done at this present time exactly as it was eight centuries ago is one that staggers the mind of the modern man, who, together with his belief in God, cherishes also a belief in progress and evolution. As a Carthusian lived in the years immediately after the foundation of the order, even so he now lives—"The Carthusian order was never reformed because it never became deformed." For eight long centuries that life has gone on unchanged. This order and the other great contemplative orders are centers of life; apparently inactive, their members forever put forth the truly mighty act, the act of prayer. Less than ever can we do without them today: their existence is a necessity. They are on the towering summits. They form a girdle of fortifications against the powers of evil. They are great white fires, forever burning in sacrifice to God.

The Carthusian lives in his cell as solitary as a hermit. Solitude is the monk's dwelling place and his lifelong home. Solitude closes him in, even as Jesus dwells in the Tabernacle. There everything breathes silence. Like a whirlpool, this silence covers him and carries him toward calm and infinite heights beyond the reach of any storm.

All Carthusian monasteries are in places of deep silence and solitude: on a mountain summit, in a valley among mountains like La Valsainte, in the middle of a wood, on a high tableland. Over their roofs blows the wind of unbroken silence.

These places hum like hives of the spirit; nothing is to be heard, but the atmosphere is full-charged with power. To every quarter of the world the invisible stream flows forth, the Spirit which comes from God and passing through these open souls fares forth in every direction. The life of the Carthusians passes in a high, powerful rhythm. Their day is like a lovely, clean line, where everything falls into its own place: the day fits perfectly into the week, the week into the

month, the month into the year, the year into the
century, and the century into eternity. The purpose of
every act, every gesture, every silence is to dwell close
to God. This is not achieved by painful striving with
rigid and overstrained will. It comes as freely as the
blossoms high up on the orchard trees. There are
storms, too, and bitter trials: God wants all the fruit.
But there is peace, and goodness. . . . *O Bonitas!*

In our near-sighted view, this life may seem a foolish
impossibility and a mutilation of man's nature, and yet
to live in this way, hidden with God in the silence, is
really the highest and the mightiest attainment. That
is why these monks have chosen this solitude. "Now
just consider for yourselves," it says in the *Consuetu-
dines* which have been crystallized into their Rule,
"how greatly the solitary life developed the minds of
the holy and venerable Fathers Paul and Anthony,
Hilarion, Benedict and others, too many for us to
enumerate; and you will have proved that the sweet
thrills of psalmody, the study of lessons, the fervor of
prayer, the subtleties of meditation, the raptures of
contemplation, the baptism of tears can be fostered by
nothing better than by solitude."

In his Bull of July 8, 1924—in which the statutes
of the Order of Carthusians are reconsidered in ac-
cordance with the demands of the new code of canon
law and reaffirmed—Pope Pius XI stated anew the
pre-eminence of the contemplative life in general and
of the Carthusian Order in particular:

"All those who have taken the vow to lead a solitary life far from the tumult and foolishness of the world, not only that they may train the whole power of their spirit upon the contemplation of the divine mysteries and the eternal verities and may offer to God incessant prayer for the unfolding and expansion, ever wider and wider, of His Kingdom, but also that they may expunge and offer recompense for their own and their neighbors' sins and shortcomings by the mortifications of body and soul defined and laid down in the Rule—all such, like Mary of Bethany, have without doubt chosen the better part.

"One can set before man for his choice and his desiring no more perfect state or way of life than this, if so be that God calls a man thereto; through their inward sanctity, they who are so nearly joined to God do in very truth, in the solitary, still life of the cloister, work in powerful sort together with Him to keep bright the radiance of holiness which the unspotted Bride of Christ presents before all mankind, that beholding they may follow. . . .

"Perhaps there are still some who hold the opinion that the virtues so unjustly called 'passive' have long since become obsolete, and that we should allow the ancient monastic discipline to be replaced by the freer and less binding practice of the 'active' virtues. This opinion has been refuted and condemned by Leo XIII. . . . Indeed, it is plain to be seen that they who dedicate themselves without respite to the service of prayer and penance, do much more for the progress of the Church and the salvation of mankind than they who labor to cultivate God's fields, since, if they provided not the channel whereby the abundance of Divine Grace might descend upon those fields, they who labor to sow the Gospel seeds would reap but scanty fruits of their labor. . . .

"Like a good tree, planted by the right Hand of God in the field of the Church Militant, to bring forth continuously the fruits of righteousness in abundance, such is the Carthusian Order."

6

A CARTHUSIAN SPEAKS . . .

ALL life is fraught with mystery both in its origin and in its workings. Thus the spiritual life, which is the most mysterious of all, life's very essence, is the most hidden and least explicable; for it is too simple and too infinite, preventing words and beyond expression.

Those who have spoken of it have usually been compelled to deal only with its outward aspects, so as to be understood by the world: the full beauty of the King's Daughter has remained hidden. The contemplative life is in reality an activity simple in itself; but it can be viewed from more than one angle, according as one considers its way of expression, its results, and those outward fruits it bears which are more or less visible and tangible; or, taking the opposite course, as one penetrates to its inner, esoteric being, which is inaccessible to aught but pure Love.

Outwardly the life of a contemplative monk has in it guarantees which are as ramparts against sin and the world, the walled garden where his soul dies and flowers again. The first effect of this, and the one which has received perhaps the most attention, is the sanctification of the monk himself, since his life becomes fuller and more harmonious. It is a known fact, too, that this life overflows and pours itself out over the world of souls, thus having as its second, wider and nobler effect the stirring up of souls to receive grace, through the might of sacrifice and prayer. But even this is only a radiation of the unitive life; it is not its center and focus. What then is the point of origin and the final goal, the inexhaustible food and the unwavering purpose of the religious life, and more especially of the Carthusian life? Presently we will try to explain this, or at any rate to give some idea of it. But first we must say a few words both about the outward conditions under which this life develops, and about those additional results which the world in some degree admits, or at least does not flatly deny.

Mortification of the senses by a strict rule of life, mortification of intellect and will by obedience, mortification of the whole man by solitude—these are the ramparts and fosses behind which he entrenches himself, who has been chosen out by Grace. The three practices thus briefly indicated make up what is usually called "Carthusian penance." To be sorry for the life one has lived; to be converted, that is, to turn from the world and direct one's way toward God: this is the first step in the Carthusian life, as in every religious life; with this act we begin this life. Those whom the divine Voice calls to the solitude of our cloisters have heard the words of the Gospel: "Do penance"; and: "Go, sell whatsoever thou hast." Above all, they have set before themselves the task of detaching themselves from all created things, of breaking the chains of our bondage. The acts of detachment, strictness toward oneself, and submission are and always have been required of a life dedicated to the worship of Him who has naught to do with things that are not.

These practices are most certainly essential for the development of the *vita unitiva*—the life of union. Unfortunately, they are almost all that the majority of mankind knows about the contemplative orders, and most hagiographers have comprehended little more in the lives of the saints. For the better understanding of these practices, and to prevent the continuance of a mistaken idea that is only too often met with, it will be useful to state at once that physical penitential practices are always of a *negative* and *relative* nature: negative, because they have no value whatsoever in themselves, their function being merely to clear certain obstacles from the path; relative, because, if they are to be not barren but fruitful, they must be brought into relationship with their inner purpose, divine Love and union with the divine Life. Hence it is clear that these practices, as they are carried on in the contemplative orders, these acts of a Serapion or a Suso, cannot of themselves afford a criterion by which to judge those who practice them. And it is a like mistake to look upon them as an end in themselves, or to think that our ideal is expressed by them. The spirit of the Carthusian statutes is very plain on this point, and their meaning is made perfectly clear. In this, more than in any other monastic order, penance is made subordinate to contemplation, in a moderate and wise ordering. The bodily severities, fixed and regulated by our Fathers, are recommended only on condition that they are undertaken under guidance, as a part of obedience. Obedience must itself be the spontaneous result of humility, and so of that charity in which alone true detachment can be brought to complete perfection and the heart's bonds loosened.

PERSONAL SANCTIFICATION: A BY-PURPOSE

According to the belief of most people, sanctification of self is the goal toward which the Carthusian strives. To prune and purify the soul; to ennoble it by the practice of the virtues, patiently exercised, vivified and nourished in the forcing-house of the monastery; in order to taste at last the pure blessedness of living and dying in the Law of the Lord—surely this is more than enough to justify a man in giving up the world, and very likely some of those who come to the solitude have no wider or deeper desire.

THE WINNING OF SOULS: A BY-PURPOSE

Yet many are conscious within themselves of a more universal mission: dead to themselves, they wish to bear fruit, like the ear of corn spoken of in the twelfth chapter of the Gospel according to Saint John. They wish to work for the salvation of souls, to be apostles and send forth light over the world by the powerful, hidden act of prayer and sacrifice.

This is a very lofty purpose and surely worthy of a soul's devotion, and yet it does not contain the blissful secret which is the first principle and essence of our life. At the beginning of our spiritual journey most of us are drawn toward the realm of these desires, but gradually we come to know that this is not the Promised Land, and to feel that we are called to possess a more hidden, a more real and a purer Eden. If one of us were to go no further than this secondary goal, he would not be able to experience the fullness of his calling, and because he had not aimed at the heavenly Target, the Divine Heart, it might very well happen that he would in like degree have failed to fulfill, to the point to which God's grace called him, the mission to which he thought it his duty to devote himself. For this is the law of conquest, and above all of spiritual conquest. To attain to the lofty goal, enfeebled fallen man lacks one single quality, the holy audacity to aim high enough, to dare to draw at the zenith the slack bow of his love and faith. He who with a single heart desires the righteousness of the Kingdom of God receives also in full measure the crown of glory, and to him it is granted to dispense to souls the excellent wine of triumph from the Eternal Feasts. But from the soul that hath aimed her

desire at self-hallowing, or any other lower goal, shall
be taken away even that for which she hath yearned.

The Aim of Aims: to Live by God Alone

To live by God alone and for God alone, that is the
heart of our secret and the true essence of our solitude.
It is also the one condition of our victory: for everyone who, eschewing all other, hungers and thirsts after
God alone possesses Him All in All. If we do not get
all that we ask, in spite of the express promise of Christ,
it is because we do not ask in His Name. For to ask in
His Name is naught else than to ask in God and for
God; and he whose prayer is in such measure purified
knows that he is heard in the very act of his interior
prayer. For only to long for Love is itself nothing else
than to love Love alone; then a man possesses it, and
in it all things.

God the Only Possession

To wish for nothing else, to know nothing else, to
have nothing else, but God and God alone; "to be
nothing else, so that only thou be God," to quote the
profound words of a contemplative soul: that is a just
description of the life of any soul in this place that is
true to her calling. Every other care beside this one
and only Love is superfluous. Anything that has no
part in the infinite self is too small for the human heart.

There are not many souls which have the power to

recognize the beauty of the Absolute, thus set forth; so deep have the children of Adam fallen. Rare are the souls intrepid enough to acknowledge all their weaknesses, to acknowledge their very nonentity. Rare are the souls which really dare *to be nothing*, and which, in that very act, are humble enough to be content *to be divine* and to be *sons of the Most High*, but it is precisely to this miracle of miracles that the Divine Will wishes to lead those of us who will allow ourselves to be transformed, to be in short crucified and glorified in Him. It is this unity for which the priestly prayer makes petition: "That they may be one, as we also are one . . . that they may be made perfect in one." Far, far above our scrannel holiness, our righteousness so impure that it is almost blasphemous, above even the gifts of grace with which we are enriched; above all social, all human, even all spiritual, ideals; beyond every temporal striving; in God alone: that is where life eternal begins for us even while we are still here on earth. It is not possible to formulate a "theory" of this kind of life or to express in words its essence: it is too simple. "To love," "to live in naked reality"—that is all that we can say with human words.

In order to convey some faint conception of this life, we have no choice but to make known its effects upon the soul that is swallowed up therein, and to show their relation to the theological mysteries and the life of the Church. But in so doing we are descending from the heights; we are exchanging the pure gold of silence for

A Cell Garden

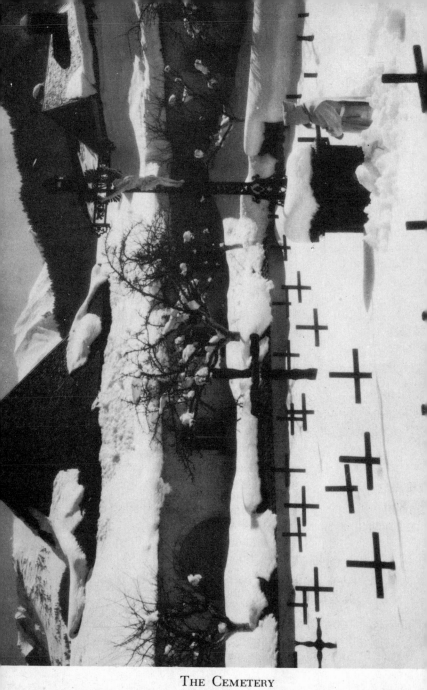

THE CEMETERY

the base metal of words. May we be forgiven the betrayal!

The Unifying of the Affective Life

Excellent things are simple things, and true life, the life of union, is the simplest of all. The soul comes, so to say, within the range of a holy spell, so that it is no longer in a position to desire any created thing, but is reduced to immobility by the exceeding great joy of Love. A peace that passes understanding flows forth from this submission and from the state of equilibrium in which the heart now feels itself to be established. For a long time more, until its transformation is perfected, the soul that is made one with its God doubtless commits faults and registers relapses, at any rate in appearance. But these very imperfections become occasions of love, and feed the flame wherein the gazing heart has its permanent abode. Its own frailties amaze not nor hinder it, no more than do its virtues, for it has arrived at the meeting place of two infinites, its own infinite need for mercy and the infinite mercy of God. From the bottomless abyss where these two abysses meet, the heart unwearyingly draws up, like water, both the humble trust and the clear, calm thankfulness which fused together are the perfect hymn of praise.

The Unifying of the Intellectual Life

Just as the will, in one only possession, possesses all things, even so the understanding, in possessing one single truth, possesses all the treasures of wisdom and of knowledge. This ultimate unification, which in a certain sense comes of itself, is not the least of the mysteries of the inner life. Then the following words acquire a glory and a brightness which the world knows not: You know all things because you are Christ's. "All things whatsoever I have heard of my Father, I have made known to you." In anticipation and in participation this is already that life of the understanding which is forever sunk in the Divine knowledge, and which, in the uncreated Word, beholds all intelligible entities and their intelligible relationships. What name can be given to the gentle, powerful light that is born in the innermost part of the soul as soon as we have received Christ into ourselves? It has no name: it is the Light that lighteth every man coming into this world, and that so few accept. All things live in this Light, and all things have been made by this Light. At bottom all things are only light rays of one Fire, and this Fire longs but to consume our hearts. Love, and you will know all things, for you will understand that all things are but the shadow cast by Love.

The Unifying of the Spiritual Life

By union with God and the reversion of the soul's faculties to Unity, simplification is obtained both of will and of intellect, and by that very act they are perfected. For in the eternal order "simple" means "perfect."

The spiritual life properly so called goes the self-same way and is perfected at the selfsame point. The "devotions" in which the soul's faculties, at the beginning of the life of prayer, seek varying degrees of diversion are now all bent in one direction. The "practices" have reverted to one single act of infinite value, which is not so much done by, as accomplished in, the soul. For this act is entirely a divine act. It consists in our allowing God to be in us. It can be called love, faith, trust, worship, sacrifice for sin, thanksgiving: the words are all synonymous, and their concepts seem, like subsidiary substances, to melt and fuse together in the glowing crucible of a heart in which living Love itself is burning.

Various Aspects of the Goal When Attained

The soul to which it has been granted to despise the world and to despise itself to the point of entire self-oblivion—or, to go to the root of the matter, the soul which possesses the ability to see as nothing everything that is nothing—such a soul, being detached from itself, sees how the Divine Wisdom supplants its selfhood. When the image of every creature and all limited desires have been swept away by the continuous trials which have purified it, then it becomes that spotless mirror whereof Solomon speaks, the Face of the Father is reflected in it, and it is identified with Him in glory incomprehensible, and Love ineffable.

The life of the soul has been absorbed into the Life

Divine: "The Lord thy God is a consuming fire." The Word became flesh to communicate to us this Fire: "I am come to cast fire on the earth: and what will I, but that it be kindled?" And in an excess of love it has drawn the soul to itself: "I have loved thee with an everlasting love, therefore have I drawn thee, taking pity on thee."

By absorbing the soul, it has transformed it. And thus, in the soul which has been conformed to the likeness of Christ, the Father finds His Beloved Son.

The ultimate purpose of our life and its total significance are comprehended in this: that in us God may know Himself and take His delight. "This is my beloved Son, in whom I am well pleased." The soul, love's adept now and swallowed up in Love, hears these words uninterruptedly, and with the Son it repeats incessantly, "I do always the things that please him."

We have been selected from out of the world and called to the secret garden of solitude for the good pleasure of God, to assuage the inexpressible thirst of Love rejected. These thoughts are beyond the range of our minds and hearts, and there is no hope at all of our being understood by those to whom no such experience has come. And yet, the Father created men only that He might find His Christ in them; simply and solely to this end. He seeks Christ in mankind. He desires to stir up, to love and to glorify in us His image and likeness, His Word, in short, Himself.

But mankind is deaf to this call; he draws away from

God's kiss. And so Love shut out, Love suppliant, Love crucified, has chosen certain souls from among the weakest and the poorest, to take comfort at least in them.

God is Love. Thus He wills and can will only Love, and the divine thirst of Jesus can be assuaged only by love. To comfort Jesus; to let God's will be fulfilled in us; among thankless mankind to be Christs, in whom the Father may live and perfect His adorable work— that is the mystery of our calling.

To receive Jesus; to afford a refuge to "the son of man (who) hath not where to lay his head"—"But as many as received him, he gave them power to be made the sons of God, to them that believe in his name. Who are born, not of blood, nor of the will of the flesh, nor of the will of man, but of God." In the soul that gives itself over to Him and consents to the total sacrifice in which all love finds fulfillment, God quickens His Word. Such a soul belongs no more to the generations of earth; it is no longer the daughter of the flesh, nor of its own will, but it is born of God in the fullness of every moment. Its life is drawn from the Divine Life; it knows God with the knowledge wherewith He knows Himself; it loves Him with the love wherewith He loves Himself; it has become Truth, perfected praise; it is uttered with the Word. In short, it corresponds to the pattern contained from all eternity in the blessed Being of God; it is simply that which God wills. In it are confirmed the prophetic words of the holy Books: "This is my rest for ever and ever: here will I dwell, for I have chosen it." "And the bridegroom shall rejoice over the bride, and thy God shall rejoice over thee."

Thanks to those hearts that are reborn in love, Christ continues to live upon earth, and to suffer for the salvation of men and the glory of the Father; for they may in very truth say: "And I live, now not I; but Christ liveth in me." And, because of this transformation of personality, it is proper for them too to say: "Our conversation is in heaven." They know too the inner meaning of the following words: "Blessed are the clean of heart." "He that seeth me seeth the Father also." "And this is the will of my Father that sent me: that every one who seeth the Son, and believeth in him, may have life everlasting." "I will that where I am, they also whom thou has given me may be with me; that they may see my glory which thou has given me . . . that they may be one, as we also are one: I in them and thou in me; that they may be made perfect in one."

The emanation from these hearth fires of love is incalculable, for by virtue of their union with Christ such souls are kings even as He is King. We must put it more strongly, even at risk of being misunderstood: such souls deliver the world.

Whenever a being attains to perfection by returning to the source whence it arose, it not only gains everlastingness and glorification for itself, but it also delivers other beings by communicating to them the life which it has drawn up from the wellspring of its own being. Whenever a plant, for example, is at one with the source of its being, it grows and comes into full possession of the beauty for which it was made. But at the same time it bears fruit, brings forth seeds, and propagates in time and space the life of its kind, and so becomes, in some sort, an agent for the delivery of its brethren of the plant world. Even so is a sanctified soul. It has no care but to unite itself closely with the very Source of all things. In this union it not only gets for itself all the beauty of which it is capable, but it also becomes universal.

By acting only in and through God the man of prayer puts himself at the center of all hearts; he influences all; he gives to all of the fullness of the grace which he knows and by which he is possessed.

"Out of him who believeth in me, shall flow rivers of living water." In that he is fully man, the desire of mankind is fulfilled in him; as Christ, he becomes the absolute Lover, the Desired One of the eternal hills.

With how much more reason than the Latin poet can he say that he is man and that nothing human is alien to him. He has treasures stored up for every need, wine and milk for all thirst, holy balsams for all wounds. He who lies lost in the kiss of Divine Being, who lets himself be raised up with Jesus according to the Father's will, shares the breath of the Spirit, the Comforter, and becomes himself a comforter. Without moving from his place, he gives to souls of the joy eternal of which he has drunk; he lights and warms the world, because he takes thought for God alone. Isaias spoke of him when he said: "The spirit of the Lord is upon me, because the Lord hath anointed me: he hath sent me to preach to the meek, to heal the contrite of heart, and to preach a release to the captives, and deliverance to them that are shut up." Led and inspired by pure Love, he is as universal and merciful as Love itself, and like it, almighty. "Heal the sick, raise the dead, cleanse the lepers, cast out devils." "He that believeth in me, the works that I do, he also shall do; and greater than these shall he do. Because I go to the Father: and whatsoever you shall ask the Father in my name, that will I do: that the Father may be glorified in the Son."

Without doubt these things will seem like madness to the world's wisdom, for the world lives upon the passing shadows of things, while we tell you of reality, pure and eternal. The world has not the power to know either our life or our love. For our life is God; and our love is God again; and our sure, certain and perfect victory is nothing else than God Himself. God is exactly what the world knows not. Therefore the world can neither estimate the extent of our victory nor gain the slightest inkling of the victory of Christ in us. "Have confidence, I have overcome the world."

GLORIFICATION

Yet a little while and the watching and yearning of
all nature shall be satisfied through the glorification of
the sons of God. A soul that has given itself over to God
possesses this intoxicating knowledge: that the forces
opposing it and fighting against it are but mortal, that
is to say, they are not; but that He whom it has accepted
as its Friend and its Bridegroom, whom it has made its
center and its directing principle, its all and its only
one, is the One who Is. Therefore it possesses all
things, since it has given all things away: "All my
things are thine, and thine are mine." Like the apostle,
it fears neither life nor death, things present nor things
to come, powers nor principalities; for its joy is wider
than all the seas, and its peace deeper than any depth.

In order to reach, without straying and loitering,
the source of all fruitfulness, which is to be found on
the mountain heights of contemplation, the Carthusian
abases himself to the lowest depth of the abyss of not
being, where he lays upon himself absolute death of
self and total detachment from the world, thus making
actual his shining ideal:

IN SOLITUDE TO LIVE BY GOD ALONE

7

BACK IN THE WORLD

AND now, what shall I say of the return? I feel that
I have been banished from Paradise—Paradise
Relost. It is hard—ah, how hard—to come down again
to the world and its wanderings. It is heavy going, back
in the valleys where men live. I must weep to see the
world here, and to think of that other world far away
on the white heights. I am always hearing that clear
voice, saying to me: "Love is our vocation. . . ."

I look around me, and shudder at everything I see—
at myself, at the bleak lovelessness and self-satisfaction,
at the injustice done by man to man, at the incessant
blasphemy, intentional and unintentional, of God, at
the whole of our social life—for in it there is nothing
real to be found, not so much as one crumb from the
table where the feast is attended by those simple, solitary monks from whose clear eyes bright joy streams
out to meet a fellow man. A fierce agony of longing,
as for home, makes my heart cry out in pain. And yet,
the strange thing is that I have brought away with me

unmixed joy and clarity, quietness and the shining of an unassailable peace. One's eyes have been bathed in light, so that one sees sharply and with a single mind what the world is: that it is waste and void.

The God of Love loves to the end man the faithless, man the lukewarm. And one begins to understand, though it is but the first glimmer of a shadowy thought, that there is only one solution, only one way of delivery: to descend to the lowliest depth of one's own being (no chilly slime compounded from "suppressed motives," but the place of unselfing) in order that there one may lose oneself in that other depth which is God. Only in the meeting place of these two depths —"The depths cry out for the depths"—is atonement made perfect, and from there the torrents of grace stream forth over mankind, seeking for soul-depths which lie open, that it may pour itself therein.

In yonder distant place, and elsewhere on the mountain heights of contemplation, live and work the monks, meek and mighty tools in the Hand of God, God's wonderful mineworkers. Like Moses, with the rod of love undefiled they strike water from the rocks, to the sole glory of God, and solely for love of God. The miraculous is wrought by singlehearted reasonableness and absolute simplicity.

God is at hand! *O Bonitas!*

NIHIL OBSTAT:
JOHN M. A. FEARNS, S.T.D.
CENSOR LIBRORUM

IMPRIMATUR:
✠ FRANCIS CARDINAL SPELLMAN
ARCHBISHOP OF NEW YORK

August 4, 1952

The nihil obstat and imprimatur are official declarations that a book or pamphlet is free of doctrinal or moral error. No implication is contained therein that those who have granted the nihil obstat and imprimatur agree with the contents, opinions or statements expressed.